# JALEN HURTS

NFL STAR

By Douglas Lynne

Book design by Jake Nordby
Cover design by Jake Nordby

Photographs ©: Kara Durrette/AP Images, cover, 1; Ric Tapia/AP Images, 4, 7, 8–9; Roger Steinman/AP Images, 10; David J. Phillip/AP Images, 13; Aaron M. Sprecher/AP Images, 15; Albert Tielemans/AP Images, 16, 23; Perry Knotts/AP Images, 18; Kathryn Riley/AP Images, 21; Red Line Editorial, 22

Press Box Books, an imprint of Press Room Editions.

**Library of Congress Control Number: 2023909020**

**ISBN**
978-1-63494-758-9 (library bound)
978-1-63494-765-7 (paperback)
978-1-63494-778-7 (epub)
978-1-63494-772-5 (hosted ebook)

Distributed by North Star Editions, Inc.
2297 Waters Drive
Mendota Heights, MN 55120
www.northstareditions.com

Printed in the United States of America
102023

# ABOUT THE AUTHOR

Douglas Lynne is a freelance writer. He spent many years working in the media, first in newspapers and later for online organizations, covering everything from breaking news to politics to entertainment to sports. He lives in Minneapolis, Minnesota.

# TABLE OF CONTENTS

# RUNNING THE SHOW

1

Alabama fans were stunned. Starting quarterback Tua Tagovailoa went down with an injury in the fourth quarter of the 2018 Southeastern Conference (SEC) championship game. Alabama trailed the Georgia Bulldogs 28–21. Only 11:15 remained on the clock. With Tagovailoa unable to play, someone else had to step up.

**Hurts passed for 83 yards and a touchdown in the fourth quarter of the SEC championship game.**

No one had expected backup quarterback Jalen Hurts to play much. But now the Crimson Tide needed him more than ever. Hurts led a touchdown drive to tie the score. Then Alabama's defense made a clutch stop. Hurts and his offense got the ball back with just over three minutes to play.

Alabama could only push ahead two yards on its first two plays. Then on third and eight, Hurts stood strong in the pocket. He delivered a deep pass to tight end Irv Smith Jr. for a first down.

Soon, Alabama was just 15 yards away from the end zone. Hurts took the snap and dropped back. Then he found a lane to run.

### COMING OFF THE BENCH

Jalen Hurts was Alabama's backup quarterback for the entire 2018 season. But he was still involved in the team's offense. Between running and passing, Hurts recorded 932 yards and 10 touchdowns in 13 games.

Hurts scored the winning touchdown on a 15-yard run late in the fourth quarter.

**Hurts (2) celebrates with his team after winning the 2018 SEC championship.**

He scrambled quickly to the goal line, where he had just one man to beat. Hurts powered through him and tumbled into the end zone with 1:04 remaining in the game. He pounded

his chest in celebration as his teammates surrounded him.

Hurts's performance helped Alabama win the SEC title with a 35–28 victory. His team was going to the 2018 College Football Playoffs.

BAMA

# DUAL THREAT

2

Jalen Hurts was born on August 7, 1998, in Houston, Texas. He grew up in Channelview, a small town east of Houston. Jalen's father, Averion, inspired him to play sports. And it was clear that Jalen had unique athletic skills.

Jalen began powerlifting at Channelview High School. However, he really shined on the football field. Jalen overwhelmed defenses with his mix of

**Hurts led Alabama to the national championship game in his first year of college.**

runs and passes. Many big-name colleges wanted Jalen to be their quarterback.

Hurts decided to play for the University of Alabama. Their team was already a powerhouse in college football. Hurts would get to test his abilities against some of the best up-and-coming athletes in the sport. And he didn't disappoint. In 2016, Hurts became Alabama's starting quarterback in the second game of his freshman year.

He led Alabama to a 14–0 record before facing Clemson for the national title. Hurts did it all in that game too. He tossed a touchdown. He also scored on a 30-yard run. However, Alabama couldn't hold on to beat Clemson. The Crimson Tide lost a thrilling game, 35–31.

In 2017, Alabama had another chance at the national title. Hurts's talent was the talk

**Hurts (2) supported Tua Tagovailoa (13) and helped him become a better quarterback.**

of college football. But Alabama fell behind 13–0 to Georgia in the national championship game. Hurts was benched. Tua Tagovailoa led Alabama to a 26–23 win in overtime.

Hurts couldn't win back the starting job in 2018. Even so, he remained loyal to his team. He trained hard to be ready for another chance. He got one in the SEC championship game.

Hurts looked unstoppable in the fourth quarter as he rallied his team to victory. Alabama made it to the national championship game but lost to Clemson 44–16.

Hurts knew he was good enough to be a starter. So in 2019, he transferred to the University of Oklahoma. He led his new team to a Big 12 title. And he had such a good season that he was the runner-up for the Heisman Trophy. This award is given to the best player in college football. Hurts made big plays look easy, especially with his legs. That ability caught the attention of many teams in the National Football League (NFL).

## PATIENTLY WAITING

Jalen Hurts's positive attitude never changed, even after he was benched. He supported Tua Tagovailoa from the sidelines. Hurts cheered for him—and the team—to be successful. Hurts said that his time on the bench taught him the value of patience.

Hurts led the Oklahoma Sooners to a 12-2 record in his senior year of college.

EAGLES
2

3

# NEW-AGE PLAYER

NFL teams didn't know if Hurts's skills would be a good fit for the professional level. In the NFL, quarterbacks typically focus on passing rather than running. The Philadelphia Eagles gave Hurts a chance. They selected him 53rd overall in the 2020 NFL Draft.

In Week 13 of his rookie season, Hurts became the team's full-time starter. The

**Hurts is hard to defend because he can throw or run every time he has the ball.**

**Hurts threw for 258 yards in his first playoff game, a 31–15 loss to the Tampa Bay Buccaneers.**

NFL learned quickly that his abilities were a great fit for the pro game.

In 2021, the Eagles hired a new head coach, Nick Sirianni. His style of offense fit perfectly with Hurts's dual-threat ability. Hurts became a star. He finished the regular season with excellent passing and rushing numbers. His

784 rushing yards and 10 rushing touchdowns led all NFL quarterbacks.

However, Hurts and the Eagles didn't look as good in the playoffs. Hurts threw two interceptions and lost a fumble in a Wild Card loss. Hurts blamed himself. He said he wasn't yet the leader his team needed. In the offseason, he focused on his communication and his throwing accuracy.

The Eagles opened the 2022 season soaring. Hurts led Philadelphia to the first 8–0 start in team history. He finished the season with a 14–1 record as a starter. He was also named a Pro Bowl starter and an MVP finalist. But he

## DAY OF CARE

In 2022, Jalen Hurts went on an eight-hour tour of Philadelphia. He called it his "Day of Care." Hurts made four stops to mentor young students. He talked to them about working hard, chasing their dreams, and the importance of a good education.

wasn't done yet. He led the Eagles through the playoffs and into the Super Bowl.

The game started exactly as the Eagles had hoped. Hurts made big plays all over the field. Heading into halftime, his team had a 24–14 lead over the Kansas City Chiefs.

However, Philadelphia's hope turned to heartbreak. The Chiefs kicked a last-second field goal to defeat the Eagles 38–35. The loss was painful. But Hurts finished with the most rushing yards (70) and rushing touchdowns (3) by a quarterback in Super Bowl history. The future looked bright for Hurts and the Eagles.

### JALEN HURTS
### CAREER PASSING STATISTICS

- **2020** – 1,061 yards, 6 TDs, 4 interceptions
- **2021** – 3,144 yards, 16 TDs, 9 interceptions
- **2022** – 3,701 yards, 22 TDs, 6 interceptions

Hurts dives across the goal line to score a touchdown during the Super Bowl.

# TIMELINE MAP

1. **Houston, Texas: 1998**
   Jalen Hurts is born on August 7.
2. **Channelview, Texas: 2016**
   Hurts finishes his high school career as one of the country's top dual-threat quarterbacks.
3. **Tuscaloosa, Alabama: 2016**
   On September 10, Hurts takes over as Alabama's starter. He becomes the first true freshman quarterback to start for the school in 32 years.
4. **Tampa, Florida: 2017**
   Hurts and Alabama lose 35–31 to Clemson in the national title game on January 9.
5. **Atlanta, Georgia: 2018**
   On December 1, Hurts leads Alabama to a 35–28 comeback win in the SEC championship game.
6. **Norman, Oklahoma: 2019**
   Hurts plays his first game for Oklahoma on September 4, putting up 508 yards in a 49–31 win.
7. **Bronxville, New York: 2020**
   On April 24, the Philadelphia Eagles select Hurts 53rd overall in the NFL Draft.
8. **Glendale, Arizona: 2023**
   Hurts and the Eagles battle the Kansas City Chiefs in Super Bowl LVII on February 12. Despite Hurts's record-setting performance, the Chiefs win 38–35 on a last-second field goal.

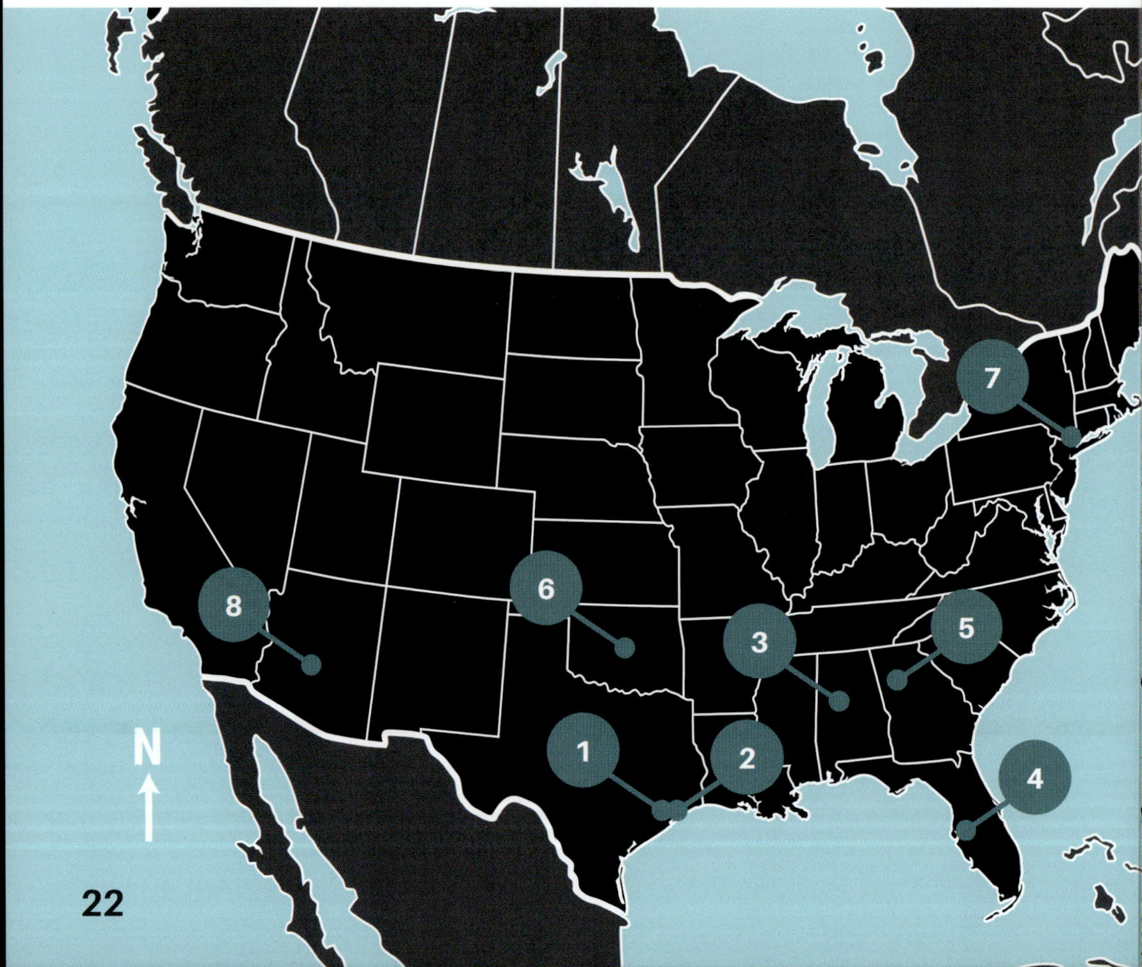

# AT-A-GLANCE

## JALEN HURTS

**Birth date:** August 7, 1998

**Birthplace:** Houston, Texas

**Position:** Quarterback

**Height:** 6 feet 1 inch

**Weight:** 223 pounds

**Current team:** Philadelphia Eagles (2020–)

**Past teams:** Alabama Crimson Tide (2016–19), Oklahoma Sooners (2019–20)

**Major awards:** SEC Offensive Player of the Year (2016), SEC Freshman of the Year (2016), First-team All-SEC (2016), College Football Playoff National Champion (2017), First-team All-Big 12 (2019), Pro Bowl (2022), Second-team All-Pro (2022)

*Accurate through the 2022 season.*

# MORE INFORMATION

To learn more about Jalen Hurts, go to **pressboxbooks.com/AllAccess**.

These links are routinely monitored and updated to provide the most current information available.

# GLOSSARY

### draft
An event that allows teams to choose new players coming into the league.

### dual-threat
Having to do with a quarterback who can both pass and run effectively.

### powerlifting
A sport in which an athlete lifts as much weight as he or she can.

### runner-up
Second-place finish.

### scrambled
Ran with the football (as a quarterback) instead of passing it.

### transferred
Changed schools to play for a different team.

# INDEX